Tilting at Time

Also by Greg Tome and published by Ginninderra Press
Watching from the Shadows

Greg Tome
Tilting at Time

With thanks to Ron Pretty for his guidance and support regarding the poems selected for this book.

Thanks also to Anna Kerdijk Nicholson, Rhiannon Hall and Peter Lach-Newinsky for their continued guidance and support, and to the members of poetry group in the Fellowship of Australian Writers, Southern Highlands, NSW.

To Norma, Erica, Matthew and Penny

'Lone Tree Silhouette' was first published in *Wild* (Ginninderra Press, 2018)

Tilting at Time
ISBN 978 1 76041 783 3
Copyright © text Greg Tome 2019
Cover photo: Matthew Tome

First published 2019 by
GINNINDERRA PRESS
PO Box 3461 Port Adelaide 5015 Australia
www.ginninderrapress.com.au

Contents

I want…	7
This is the time	8
4 a.m. ruminations	10
5.15 Summer Morning	11
Moonlit magic	12
Possum pendulous	14
Musings of a philosophic rabbit	16
Gastropod aeronaut	17
Lone tree silhouette	18
Eucalyptus Rex	19
Lemon tree	21
Fuchsia future	22
Woman swimming with fish	23
Poseidon meets Woopi	25
My Byzantium	27
Motoring into memory	29
Bowral landscape	32
Autumnal variations	34
Partly cloudy day	36
Winter winds	37
Matinee	38
Chamber orchestra concert	39
Classic cleansing	41
Trailing Titinius	43
Red dot romance	46
Companionship vicissitude	47
Prince Albert never washed up	48
The lives of others	52
Rialto calling – a man who has nothing	54
Made in China	56

The new religion	60
The Road to Damascus	63
Refugee camp	64
Position vacant for a deity	66
Jet fighter trails	69
Life story	70
God knows	73
An aching gap	75
Lingua lashing	78
Prayer of an insomniac	80
Waiting room ritual	82
Messotopia	86
Recovering health in a funambulist manner	88
Senior Time	90
Inarticulatus dotageous	91
Song of a retiree	93
Saturday morning	95
Proposals for the afterlife	96

I want...

I want words that dance
    that sing
        that shine light into hidden crevices
                expose fires
                          that smoulder
                    under seemingly calm surfaces

I want words that whisper secrets to me
                  known only to a few
        words that re-tell stories long forgotten
                that touch tender spots usually ignored

I want words that grip
            and hold and shake
                will accept no denying
    words that mutter
             that shout
                squeeze my heart
              sear my brain
    words that haunt
        returning
            to bother
                to pester
  time
      and time and time again

I want words
      and words
            and more words

I want
    to be a poet

This is the time

Now

    when the shameless day covers her limbs
        distractions
          and demands
            fade

    when the tired brain
        rejects the morning's
            pretentious notions

    when an outer
      and inner stillness
         ushers in those images
            that linger
              and please
              or tease

    when sleep flees
      behind a curtain
         beyond the grasp
            of likelihood

    when the sadness of the night
        filters the dross
            from the day's stories
      and an eerie beam
        bent through the prism
          of this special time
        lights up the skeletons
        of obscure truths

```
          when an impudent virus
                      insists
                 that this and this
            has to be    stated   or
written
       or
            recorded
                         somehow

Then this is the time
            to write poetry
```

4 a.m. ruminations

More wide awake than ever
        scripting my interview with Penny Wong
    rehearsing the number plates of cars
            owned decades ago
    sensing the humid air pushed in
        from outside
        by the ever punctual drizzle

Parts of my battered old body
        long ignored
    take the opportunity to remind me
            that they still exist
    would like to be acknowledged

I wrestle with the possibility of sleep
    but it seems miles away
        giving way to pop ups
            of opening lines of various poems
        most of which will wither
            while in embryonic form

Inevitably the time arrives
    I succumb to the lure
            of a book on a table
                in another room

I agree to the terms of surrender
    the donning of a warmer garment
        the Genesis-like inundation by light
    the knowledge that the following day
        will be shattered into chunks of lethargy

5.15 Summer Morning

Somewhere in the distance
    a rooster auditions
        for the role
            of a comic Pavarotti
Much closer
    an array of birds
        parody *Question Time*
            aggressively
A hint of the heat to come
    seeps into the bedroom
        where ancient aches
    are wrapped in apprehension
For a moment
    a sense of awe quiets
        the prattling birds
A new day shakes itself
    before emerging from its kennel

Moonlit magic

Moonlight spreads wide
       across its share of the planet
Clouds
    agents of ignorance
         fight to block its sweep
    but its magical influence
         eventually wins through

With a touch of unsurpassed mystery
       moonlight converts rocks into garden plants
         while flowers become rocks
The mutual transubstantiations
         are happily accepted
Come daylight the process will be reversed

Under its light touch
       trees assume an added majesty
    solid stone buildings
         wear a coat of lightness and welcome
Such gentle trickery is never resented

Aged and desperate witnesses to these visits
         by such a congenial otherworld
       inhale the optimism
            cramming the air
    shedding temporarily the tiresome companionship
         of aches and fears

Morning
    skating in on cynical daylight's aversion
                          to such niceties
                                ends it all

But only for the time being

Keenly awaited
    but soon enough
    moonlight will again flow
        over the horizon parapet
      to blanket our world
      in its special embrace

Possum pendulous

At first glance
        a pathetic imitation of a dead branch
    there he has hung for months
        tangled in electric wires
            high above the roadside
A most forlorn messenger
    he advertises mortality
        to all who happen to glance up

Akin to criminals
    in days long past
        in another country
            whose desiccated bodies
                purveyed a ghoulish welcome
                to any passing the town limit
    his crime one of impetuosity
        that characterised his lifestyle
    a lesser fault
        but with similar dire consequences

His boisterous lifestyle
    has come to this
        now ending his bouncing off metal roofs
    fighting off male rivals
        assaulting the night's silence
            with a cacophonous hissing
    sleeping the day through
        in some haven
            beyond the hegemony of any dog

The wind sways his body
    in a sad mimicry of life
Soon the time will come
    when he shall fall to the ground
        his purgatory sentence ended
           with his duty to remind humans
               of their temporary loan
               of time on earth

Musings of a philosophic rabbit

Fading light tugs me out from acacia shelter
past where my sometime love lies mashed
on the road, onto flat vacant paddocks scattered
over with sweet tussocks. When their nearness
threatens, my quick dash from cover to cover
startles walking couples. Later dense dark guards
me, guides me to yards where no dog treads;
lettuce, parsley abound. Away from harsh
bushland, away from the wile of fox, urban life
cossets me. Here I fight the irk of possums,
pampered creatures stamped native by accident
of parting continents. My kind, benevolent conquerors
of how to live in this land, face scorn unfrayed
by the centuries – the fate of later-comers
of all kinds to this place.

Gastropod aeronaut

When I find a snail in the garden
    the Buddhist in me
        forbids me crushing it underfoot
But it doesn't get off scot-free
        for its trespass
Usually I chuck it onto the nearby metal roof

I wonder how it feels
        for a gastropod
           to find itself flying through the air
    before landing in some foreign field
Perhaps some life-enhancing experience
                I submit
Of a positive nature?
    Who can tell?
But life should retain its mystery
    certainly for a Buddhist
        and even for a snail.

Lone tree silhouette

Poised atop a high hill
    best viewed from a moving vehicle
   always in relationship with its own special light
it makes its stand
   capturing and fastening to itself
      for the brief duration
         the viewer's gaze
     a solitary tree

This no great giant
   straining huge limbs
      towards the sky

Discarding the company of others
   it flaunts its fragility
      exulting in its isolation
It bares for all its delicate structure
   sculptured by the most sensitive creator
Such distance deceives the viewer
   but its skeletal appearance is misleading
Those limbs are fuelled by vitality
   a genuine majesty results

Now it is gone
   disappeared from view
But never gone
     the viewer uplifted
    after such a communion

Eucalyptus Rex

Gum trees all around
Gum trees in my heart

Great stretches of our land
        exult in their embrace

Gum trees in my brain
I see great clumps of them
        white trunks and stooped shoulders
            gathered in tightly knit gossipy groups

I see black-trunked skinny legged
        tribes of them
        pushed together as if preparing
        for a corroboree
        in harmony with the first of our kind
        to cherish them

Then there are the tall ones
        that demand you stand back
            run your eyes up their grand height
            from base to very top

Allow your soul to follow your gaze
        drink in the majesty of their bearing
Feel the otherworldliness of being so high
        sharing another realm with the birds
        who carry their privilege
            with soaring dignity

I acknowledge there are other trees here
    migrants that prefer a pampered existence
        away from the hardship of open country
After a period of shameless nakedness
    they don the brightest colours
            flaunted in some Rio parade
But the carnival soon ends
    and they retire into unexceptional verdure

No need for showy display for gum trees
    their toying with colour is more restrained
        rooted in the confidence
            that this is their land
Before us all
    they were here
    and their olive-grey dominance will continue
        long
    long
        after all interlopers
            are gone

Lemon tree

You can't treat a lemon tree
    as you would a mistress
        lavishing it with occasional gifts
Nor should you abandon it
        because of its fading looks
For your loyalty and constancy
        it repays you many times over
But spoil it with too much kindness
        and it plays upon your weakness
Underneath its raiment of shiny green
    menacing thorns await
        for a presumptuous hand
            groping for its fruit

Sometimes a mistress
    would be less demanding

Fuchsia future

I'd like to return to earth as a fuchsia
Being something colourful
    after a long life
        as a big boofy human male
            devoid of any brightness for the eye
    would be a pleasant change
I'd still have a quiet resilience
    and be able to survive tough times
        knowing that every spring
            I could flaunt my particular majestic display
        that would last long into late summer

Such worries as how to spell my name correctly
    would now elude me

Sprung originally from somewhere in the Caribbean, perhaps
    I would exult in my exotic beginnings
        no matter where I grew
That could be anywhere on the planet
    a sort of surprise overseas holiday

Perhaps because of some remnant of big boofy male memory
    I'd prefer my human carer to be a sensitive, dignified female
My home to be a tidy, average garden
    not some huge, ostentatious showground
We fuchsias abhor the stress of competition
    that sort of flamboyance is not our style at all

How long do fuchsias live?
    And where to after that?
I'll leave it to my fuchsia persona to decide.

Woman swimming with fish

The fish must see her
    those large lively eyes
        can't help but do so
  but they keep a respectable distance
    yet showing no concern
        for her presence.
In their piscine brains
    she is some temporary aspect of nature.
Yet there are some
      who tease
        who flirt
    weaving balletic trails
        pause
  slow   quick

There where the river consummates its destiny
    becoming one with the sea
  and the tide attains a magical height
    they arrive.
First the fish
    then her,
  the retinue preceding
      the intriguing visitor.

Every time
    the initial caress of water
        wraps her in a tactile envelope
            a cocoon that moves with her
                as she strokes evenly in obeisance
        to the demands
    of being allowed into this liquid kingdom.
She leaves when eventually
            the water's cosseting hands dull –
    the fish do nothing
        to mark her departure.
As she choreographs her way
            into the bale of fiery air
              her car's interior
    she savours the aftermath
        of comfortably tired bones
            and tingling skin.
But there is more
        another sensation
             elusive like her fishy companions
  yet real
    long lasting
  a sense of sharing another world
    like the confluence of river and ocean
        it stretches beyond
            her day to day existence.

Poseidon meets Woopi*

* aka Woolgoolga

Monstrous chunks of broken-edged chocolate blocks
    carelessly rock line the land's edge
  resisting Poseidon's relentless tongue
      licking at their existence

Further out
    introverted outcrops skulk
      in their defiant attempts
        to break the horizon's dominance

An arc of low clouds hover
  as a guard of honour
Or is it a vanguard
    of some invading force?

The bordering land hosts
    a miscellany of bushes
      bowing and twisting
  to avoid being noticed
    as if lacking passports or citizenship

Other trees
    confident of their right
      to be exactly where they are
  stand etched sharply
    against the background of the ever moving sea

While plovers and wagtails
    noisily berate the world
  gulls dive and swoop
    adding their own characteristic squawk
      to the news of the world
That done
    they settle for group companionship
      each an icing sugar droplet arranged fastidiously
        atop a distant chocolate slab

My Byzantium

My weekend chaos
      to wipe away the workday routine
        of shaping the lives
    of eleven school children
        who returned the compliment

      split between two universes
          thirty miles apart

The pub at the top end of town
    my temple
      my haven
        my temporary home
  which collected to itself
      my fellow flotsam
  in our existential paradise
each shaking off his loneliness
      in his own particular method

The café where the lovely blonde Dutch girl worked
    who served me mixed grill
      offered temptation
        although it was not on the menu
      but never delivered
    substituted instead warmth
        with desire as a lingering aftertaste

      my hungry heart left unfilled

The leaden clouds that frequent the space above this town
    shoulder my thoughts into a closely packed crowd

      making appearances on stage and in court

      Ford Prefect headlights slashing through the Sunday night
        dragging me back to that other world

      the slippery mix of bonhomie and competition
           inside an aspiring cricket team

      the long wide stately street with the town's placid identity
           stamped all over it

Today
    these eyes pine as they search the town
            for some reaching out

      Did I spend all that time here once?

      What did it do to me?

Time has stealthily slid a portcullis
           between us
    an emotional barrier
    a curtain on my vision

A chunk of my life has been severed
        and sits
           a curiosity
    bereft of any meaning

So now unbalanced
    my life wobbles along
        the rest of its traced-out orbit

Motoring into memory

Grey-woolled sheep
    motionless
        heads down
    are carved rocks of granite

Bare-limbed gum trees
    pose unconcerned
        their apparel
    fallen
        around their feet

The terrain opens out
    into a more welcoming mode
Great hills have retreated
    In the distance
        they appear
    fashioned out of playdough
        by someone's overlarge children

Villages
    branded with faraway Scottish names
        – Llangollen   Ben Lomond   Glencoe
            huddle close to the road
    so close
        a feeling of daring intimacy
            concerns the passer-by
as if he has glimpsed
    some ragged underwear

In rusty idleness
    unused railway lines
        bring back memories
            of earlier
                different days

Heaped abandoned farm machinery
        serve a similar purpose
    Archaeological digs
            recording the history
                of farmworkers
                    through the years

Now different trees
        state their case
    Imported species
        remind the landowners
    there are other countries
        as they pay rigid obeisance
            in the foreign style
            of neat rows
Poplars behave similarly
    but still beg to differ
        as they flourish
            their distinctive autumn yellow

All this so fresh and interesting
        to these old eyes
    yet in years long gone
      so everyday
          they barely rated
           a notch
              on any scale

So the bite of decades
        and distance
    have hit home
  and allow me
      for a brief period
          to revisit my youth

Bowral landscape

I am beautified
>to coin a word
>primped and preened and pampered
but underneath it all
>I still have a heart

Once I was beautiful
>before men from faraway came
>>scarred my visage
>>>before subjecting me
>>>>to plastic surgery
I survived it all
>tolerating the carbuncular buildings
>>the tall pines
>>>the flowery intruders
>>>>meant for elsewhere

On clear still days
>>like some tedious blowfly
>a helicopter hangs about overhead
>>wishing to cash in on what is left
>>>of my good looks
How to overcome
>what is inflicted on me?

Time is on my side
>	as are some positives
>		from the old days
Quality will show through
>	you know
That brooding old hill to the north
>	is a case in point
>		whereas others to the west have been shaved
>			manicured into an anonymous blandness

The way you measure things
>	they'll remain thus for years
But my chronometer treats such a puny period
>	with disdain

One day long into the future
>	my beauty in all its grandeur
>		shall return

Pity you won't be here to see it

Autumnal variations

Autumn comes in many guises –
    a benign giantess
  her sturdy legs
    bare strong
  the colour of sunshine
She pushes the sky even higher
        than belief
  stills the air so clear
    as she holds her breath
      the length of the day
    air so still
      as if happily trapped
        in a giant glass jar
          clear and clean
And the changing colours
  drawn from the motley array
    of her many garments

Other times she genuflects gracefully
  covering us with her protective skirt
    as memories of the past summer
  or qualms concerning
      a fierce awaiting winter
    circle about us

Often she makes way –

        the season becomes
        the interior of a Gothic cathedral
    such space and again the stillness
Stained glass windows mesmerise
        with their pageant of colours
The hint of eternity and yearning
        entrapped within that mighty edifice
    and a sweet sadness that
        such beauty cannot last
    thought punctuated with an imagined music
    in a minor key
        that fades and fades

Sometimes there'll be intrusions
    rain and wild winds
    but for every paradise
        there has to be a netherworld

Nothing is permanent
    not even a Gothic cathedral interior
    and our delightful demi-goddess
can be tempted
    lured away to whatever attractions
        await her in a different hemisphere
despite being serenaded
    by a cicada-like chorus of lawnmowers
        beseeching her to stay
    to save them from months of redundancy

Partly cloudy day

Sunlight slashes the red mat
        inside the front door
    spills a pool on the kitchen Italian tiles
        shouts attention on the wire-ribbed bowl
            imprisoning two lemons
        that stare out at all that forbidden space

Time holds its breath
        until a cloud covers the sun
    Sunlight dons a dark coat
An army of chilled bones offers up
            a universal sigh
    which pleads to the cloud to desist

A game of see-saw continues
        light against shadow
    a scaled-down morality play
        where good and evil
           vie for power

Red mat and tiles accept what is
    lemons
        along with chilled bones
           are confused

The chilled bone owners deplore the intrusion
            of House of Reps type argy bargy
        into the daily weather pattern

Tomorrow's weather forecast
        somewhat similar

Winter winds

These winds
    bash through my heart
      batter my brain
  scatter my thoughts
    dispirit
        distract
            almost despair
                me

    Merciless
      oppressive
they drive the air
        from my being
            hope from my innards

    I wait
    I wait

    One day
      eventually
          they will ease
            they will cease

Then I expect I shall find
        my soul
            hanging forlornly
                from the branch
    of a long-dead tree.

Matinee

In the dark we struggle
    our real lives suspended
        another life, other lives
            squeeze our being

We drink in the scenery
    from this other world
We fret at the injustice
    gasp at the implausabilities
        annoy at the noise of neighbours
            govern our hopes for the ideal.

We wonder how much longer
    pray it's not too soon.
But it ends
    faint lights
        transport us out of there
            as the credits roll
We are tipped out
        into the sun washed street
            where we float between two worlds
    perhaps knowing ourselves
            a little better.

Chamber orchestra concert

The violinist and cellist hack the noise
                into solemn blocks
        or delicate slices
    The piano
        like some mythical sheepdog
            ensures cohesion
                and a way forward
The players
        both as Titans and generous Samaritans
            dominate the world

The audience
        each a pupa
               in its honeycomb cell
    isolated
        as it battles the challenges
thrust at it by the music

The inspired sound
        bulking out from the stage
rubs its back against the silence
        that blankets the rapt audience

The pupae
    grey-haired
        or bald-headed
    or with heads of tastefully dyed hair
    hold their collective breath
        as distractions
            musical themes
                or images
        fight for dominance
            in individual minds

The Titans and Samaritans
        take their bow
The pupae
    now much matured
    move about and socialise

The moment
    all those moments
        are past
But only time can trample them down completely

Their haunting powers will spring up
        at the most unexpected times
    affecting this one
        or
            that one

For many
    a visceral cleansing
        follows

Classic cleansing

We leave
The lock clicks into place
Inside the radio keeps playing
supposedly to deter
      any would-be intruders

But it must do more than that
it's classical music that plays
to the silent listening room

While we're away
as only his work can
Mozart's piano concerto
fills the space with grace
and a steely beauty
so the furniture appears tidier
the cushions elegantly fluffed up
everything in the room
takes on an easeful aura

From Russia with love
Shostakovich's swirling powerful symphony
cleans the large windows
so they glow with quiet satisfaction

Muscular heroic Beethoven
strides the floor rhythmically
striving for some ideal
while his footmarks restore
the carpet's original colour

Schubert's softer gentle passages
unobtrusively seep into the walls.

So much more
who knows how much
before we return

When we do our senses dulled
by the busyness of everyday living
yet even they suspect
a fleeting secret smile the room allows itself

Trailing Titinius

Give me some drink, Titinius – *Julius Caesar*, i.ii.127

You lead me up the garden path
                Titinius
There I was
    thinking you had but a single mention
            akin to being a spear carrier
        in Spain gently caring for a feverish Julius
your name exposed
        hovering there
        taking up a second in time
            four syllables in an iambic pentameter
then to disappear for good
        no doubt quickly forgotten
            by the audience
    only to be resurrected briefly
        at every subsequent performance

    All so neat and cosy

But you catch me out
    you sly trickster
        you were a real player
           turning up much later
              a genuine force in the action
No spear carrier this time
    but as a valued companion
        and sharing the tent
           with old Lean and Hungry himself
        while battle rages
           against the supporters
              of the butchered Caesar

Not saying much
        just fetching and carrying
                obeying orders
Then it is Cassius's turn to be confused
    wrongly believing
        you
            his best friend
        has been captured
        and killed
    he ends his own life

        So very Roman
        an act that you emulate soon after
    using his sword
        that despatched both himself and Caesar.

        In your case
    so much
and yet so little
    From a useful fringe dweller
        used to plug awkward gaps
    Modest enough
        but there is an immortality of sorts
            linked with the continued playing
                of this tragic tale

                  No more than that
           a sniff of eternity on the cheap
      Cold comfort for the name's original owner
           its existence in archives
                hidden away
                        under the thick dark skirts of time
Such little notoriety
    for a family of such import

  But to own a name that found its way
      journeying through the Bard's capacious brain
           to be tested out on his whispering lips
        to have been written by that
    distinguished hand

                    Who of us would not settle
              for such a canonisation?

Red dot romance

The switch on the power point
where I plug in the toaster
has this red dot.

It hypnotises me.
I can't escape its gaze.

When it's time to switch off
unplug the toaster
red dot and I
fix our gaze
one upon the other
long and lingering.

But click
    the dot is gone
the connection is over.

The joy from the dalliance lingers
    continues to give pleasure
but not so much
    as the taste of the toast.

Companionship vicissitude

One morning
    when I struggled out of sleep's grip
I found a tear in my pillowslip
    worn there from sharing my dreams
    over many years
The dark hours of wakefulness
    hosts to many grim memories
        aid in this fabric collapse
            as does being the custodian
                of tendernesses shared
                    with an intimate

All this gone now
        because of a miserly tear
    this faithful companion despatched
        to wherever old pillowslips go

Now I rest my head on a shiny striped piece of work
    rather virginal-looking but also somewhat ostentatious
        something like a neophyte at work
    keen to impress its employer
My dreams, my secret thoughts take some time
    to be comfortable with this unfamiliar attendant

No doubt we will get used to each other
        but to what extent is the question
    Will it be up to standard
        when the time comes to see me off
            as inevitably I go
        to wherever old worn-out pillow users go?

Prince Albert never washed up

The soothing caress on wrists
of warm water sanguine with suds,
the fulfilment of seeing a plate
pristine as a newly baptised soul
redeemed from the sins of grease –
such are pleasures the son of Saxe Coburg
and Gotha never felt.
Prince Albert never washed up.

The cousinly body of England's fresh queen
was his to explore. And explore it he did
to good effect, providing names
for Mittagong streets. Well, nine of them
at least. Names drawn from those
their children bore: Alice, Arthur, Alfred –
the list goes on. Beatrice the last
before death cut short
such paternal creativity.
In twenty years of marriage
and in all that time
Prince Albert never washed up.

Tough times chiselled at the early days
of wedded life. Anti-Teutonic sentiment
spread wide among the populace,
the denial of a title, a reduced allowance.
No wonder the prince felt peeved.
No wonder
Prince Albert never washed up.

Life's roundabout's
brought him respect
as he fought the good fight
for freeing slaves,
as he redecorated Westminster,
and guided his wife
through the dangerous shoals
of political waters.
In return she admired
his beautiful nose,
his sweet mouth and fine teeth.
No surprise then
the assembly line of children
continued. Perhaps he never had time.
Whatever the cause
he never got around to it.
Prince Albert never washed up.

When Irish actress Nellie Clifden
shared the bed of Prince of Wales,
shocked but intrepid our Albert
vacated his sick bed
while the grim reaper watched.
Albert braved the cold, braved the wet
the travel to Cambridge where Bertie
awaited a sharp fatherly tongue.
Two weeks later Albert was dead,
his queen unforgiving of young Wales,
his extracurricularities, in her eyes, a cause.
Under such circumstances
is it any wonder
Prince Albert never washed up.

Dead at forty-two
a bank of achievements
illuminates his name: better schools
across the Kingdom. The Great Exhibition
coaxed into existence
under his guiding hand.
His musical compositions
enter the repertoire.
Among all this
just one yawning gap –
Prince Albert never washed up.

Today an imposing edifice
bears his name.
Somewhere in there,
under all that splendour
must be a kitchen,
succouring snugly
a shiny sink.
Of one thing
you can be sure.
Prince Albert never entered there.
The whole thing was built
long after his death,
and besides,
Prince Albert never washed up.

The lives of others

Hand them a dog on a leash
On each side of their head
   clamp an earphone
      attached to a devilish device
         from which trickles music
            of some description
               incessant in its infusion

You have created for them
        their preferred
           otherworld
        where the footpath rolls before them
           as if featuring in some dream

Those they meet when walking
        become phantoms
     items to be tolerated
        but not valued

Other irrelevancies
        reach high into the sky
          on either side
            of parts of their path
     bending and waving in the breeze

Noisy wheeled capsules
       pass close by
     trespassing on the outskirts
        of their consciousness
           while infringing
        on their sense of convenience

The length of this state's existence
> varies for each individual

Eventually it ends
> the dog is unleashed
>> the earplugs sometimes removed

A redemption begins
> a partial return
>> to a world
>>> where others exist
> begins

Rialto calling – a man who has nothing

To be in Venice
    is to be compelled
        to visit the markets

He is already there
    sprawled on the concrete
        seemingly asleep

Over the bridge
    crossing water
        through twists and turns
    past treasure houses
        of turquoise and silver
            they come

A display of fish
    designed to catch the eye
        is caught in the camera lens

He is ignored
    not suitable material
    except for the more imaginative

Nearby keen-eyed two buy up
    tomatoes from Sicily
        local plums
            oranges from Spain
Fruits of the earth within reach of their purse
    a bonus lemon theirs for the taking

He seeks no fruit
    gets none

From China
    tentative
        clad in tight white
            two women calculate
    their manner an apology

No apology in his case
    his space is his space

Sounds of German cut the air
    a simple remark
        from father to son
    but tangible in its difference

His language is universal
        visual
    a defiant presence
        where the world
            comes to buy and sell

Made in China

Her hand is steady
        her eye straight
she guides the gibbering machine needle
            in a fast clear line
   breathes deeply with satisfaction
another shirt
     close to completion
        well ahead of target
a rough gem of a bonus
        teases from the distance
a little more money
        to be sent to honourable parents
     eking out life
        in distant hills
           of Ginshu

Her work hours are demanding
   but she has learnt to think of other things
     while her clever hands
         and sharp eye
   unrelent in their pursuit
         of a type of perfection
     crafting out
        shirt after shirt after shirt

While her thoughts make free
                to wander where they will
    a part of her
        invests the shirt
            on the machine
    with a spindly motherly love

        It seems to fill a sort of emptiness she feels.

An emotion unknown to the steel empress
    with the steely glint of a smile
        and an astonishing omnipresence
collecting and inspecting each shirt
    memorising the number
           of toilet breaks
           shirts produced

        in the dark of early morning
          prying the girls
              from their bunks
                    arranged in totalitarian orderliness
        in the factory basement

As the gestation of this shirt
                nears its conclusion
she wonders
     as if to fill a vague emptiness within her
        who will end up wearing it
she sees a western man
              fair   clean   healthy
who or where he lives
        draws an unconscious shrug
                  of her slender shoulders

              the shirt is finished

     held up for inspection
        the way a child is examined
                before being sent off to school

            such a prolific mother

Before the shirt is collected
                        more fabric left for her
        there is time for the merest celebration
Enough time to glance around
                at the rows of bent heads
        take a little comfort in the sisterhood
      which helps fill a vague ache she feels
Still enough time
            to clutch the garment gently
                  firmly
                              against her breast
        even allow the briefest brush
                against her lips
A sigh
    almost a prayer
        sending it off to a safe home.

The new religion

They say we live in a godless age
    but across great swaths
             of the spiritual landscape
        is a force creeping surreptitiously
        in a format
    that slips under the radar
             eludes recognition
is not seen for what it is
    with its claw-like grip on the devotion
            of the masses
that wears all the clothes
        of a widespread religion
The use of holy water
    supplanted by the sprinkling
            of savoury herbs

Priests and priestesses
        each soaked in charm and good health
    each with devout congregations
    perform their sacred rites
        depicted on myriad screens
           across a host of countries
    watched by reverent disciples
        following every nuance
    as they dextrously chop
measure   mix

But then in time
> as every religion has done
>> it splits into different schisms
>> carbohydrate cult jostles with protein
>>> vegan shearing off from vegetarian

Great liturgical debates
> orbit the universe
> fat   salt   sugar
> an array of oils

all have their worth
> held up to fierce canonical light
>> scrutinised and contrasted

The loyal congregations wait
> anxious for the deliberations
>> to be handed down

from

>> on

>>> high

Every epiphany greeted
> by a universal visceral sigh

The old religions stagger on
> their sacraments offering their faithful
>> grace
>>> to store up for the afterlife
> but this new one is different
>> its aim is more immediate

To have the afterlife
              a mere afterthought
   only possibly occurring
         after a long   healthy
       vitamin-packed earthly existence

The Road to Damascus

Again
the light above the road
is bright enough to blind
noise loud enough to astound.
This time
not from a divine source
but from bombs and gunfire
sent by
    would-be gods.

Not here now
a place to fall on the road
unless you're a bomb
aimed at the Assad mob
    or perhaps the ISIS
or a non-ISIS rebel group
    or an ordinary family
now labelled collateral damage.

If you're blinded by all this
don't expect to regain your sight
after three days – like last time.

From the blood and dust of this road
amongst the screams
    of the murderous metal
        those words can be heard again
addressed to each
    to all of us
        a Saul

Why persecuteth thou me?

Refugee camp

In camps like this
    they rot
By the millions
    they rot

Life is a tent
    relief an open fetid drain
Dignity fled long ago.

Food slopped grudgingly
    water measured
        rationed
            as if heavenly nectar.

Despair lives on here
        thriving in the shallow stare
    eyes bleached of joy
        by the aimless monotony of time
            flattened of any sense of rhythm.

Still more reach here
    scorn their only greeting.

Officials come
        avoid the stinking trenches
    ask questions,
        write words in official books
They go
    vehicles leaving great clouds of dust
Hope newly risen
        from the grave
            chokes in the dust

Trust
> faith in others
>> choke in the dust

Memories of home
> comfort
>> leavened with terror and madness
Some trick of fate lured them
> from there to this
> terror with madness
>> exchanged for this

Every day a taste
> of death in life.

Abandoned by any god
> they can conjure
> their only prayer
>> surely someone somewhere must care.

Position vacant for a deity

No tropical paradise this place
    but because of their god
    still they come
The steamy air is soaked
      in the odour of despair
    but because of their race
    still they come

From Myanmar agents of death
    cross the border
      seek out
        the Rohingyas or anyone else
    who try to stop them

God seems to be looking
    the other way

The rains come
    confine all to their tents
From the venerable
    oldest fortresses of civilisation
      they come
    a roll call of displaced
oppressed
      from Syria   Iraq,
    Iran   Egypt   Sri Lanka
      cluster here
    in an alliance of desperation

To them it seems
>God has taken absence
>>without leave

Here they waste away their years
>amid the heat
>>the aimless emptiness

Just sometimes the chance
>– oh so remote –
>but still a chance of somewhere else
>>lights up a dulled eye
>quickens a long torpid pulse
But such flickers of hope are rare
Makes you wonder
>if God does care

The whole area
>once green
>>lush and fertile
>has succumbed to a blanket
of hate   anger   desolation

Long ago he left us
    but still they come
To them we always say
       to each other we say
          each in his heart says to himself
             the cruel unrelenting sun
                scorching down at us
                        screams
everything
    all we hear and see
          screams out loud
    screams it so clear

                    God doesn't live here any more

Jet fighter trails

Across the visage of an immaculate sky
impossibly high above the earth
four sleek machines
        built to kill
each scores its mark
a precise chilling line of spoor
   white
       untouchable
threatening in its beauty
   in its unspoken message

       we practise to inflict death

Life story

With your 23 pairs of chromosomes
        packed into every cell
            of that body of yours
you are a walking engineering miracle
    a dazzling piece
        of imaginative design

        Such a marvel
        You must be so proud

But then again
    jaundiced eyes see you
        see all of us
            differently

    They see
        mere grains of sand
            in a vast desert
                or drops of water
                    in a huge ocean

        governed by chance
    as desert winds
        or ocean currents
            chase us this way or that
our helplessness overwhelming
    in the fickleness
        of such forces

We are labelled grains
    or droplets
        in the scan of existence
            since time began

Such numbers
    from now
        to way back past Moses
    further back
    oh so far back
        to the beginning of time
  All who have ever lived
    we are placed in their midst

In the great yawn of time
    the puny amount allocated to each
      a mere flicker of an eyelid

So each of the countless desert grains
    each ocean droplet
        at some time
            alive and vital
                achock with chromosomes
            body cells
    and numerous fancy working parts
    each minute individual
        striving to live out
            their three score and ten
        is cast about disdainfully
            by fate
    and all too soon
        a momentary sad joke
            forgotten
                nameless
                    abandoned
    in the scrapheap of history

God knows

I envy poets at ease with their god
I find it hard to relate to mine
He stuffed up bigtime
        when designing humans
      prostates in men for example
birth passages for women
   appendix for both

Enough to justify a recall
        to the factory

Admittedly he did well
        creating our universe
      but it went to his head
        and he couldn't stop himself
Now there are countless universes out there
        which we'll never need

Don't mention all the cruelty   suffering
   chaos   in our world

He's not really to blame
      is he?
We want free will
     don't we?
   not a world full of robots
     as the behaviourists proffer
   or a grey landscape peopled
        with righteous civic-minded quasi-saints

Again
> the trick is in the original design of mankind
>> getting the setting just right

That is a tough call
> perhaps he got it a bit wrong
>> but who of us could have done better?

I think I should ease off being so critical
I want to be in his good books
> if we should happen to meet

An aching gap

You died long before I was born
    Somewhere there
        in the hierarchy
            of older brothers
    you fitted
        but did not stay
seemingly flitted away by chance
    from life
        as a sort of tax
            on large families
    in those hazardous days
        long gone

I know your name
        James
            but nothing else
your whole little life
        wrapped in silence
            like your tiny body
    entombed
        but away from mention
            but not memory, surely.

I know your name
> James
>> pinned to me
> as a second name
some sort of afterthought
> a vague gesture
>> to a distant memory
or perhaps
> an attempt at relief
>> from an incessant demand.

You must have lived on
> in the troubled dreams
>> of the parents we shared
> but shredded from existence
>> by the grind of farm routine
>>> until another dreaming time

Surely you re-appeared
> in the occasional what-ifs
>> of unguarded moments
> shielded from the rest of us
>> who had no way of knowing

I don't know where your grave is
> nor have I seen
>> in dusty official papers
> any details
>> of when you lived
>>> or how you died

Dismissed from family memory
    you have taken up lodgings
            in my head
Welcome
    Take your ease there
But do not stay too long
    It can be troubled territory

Lingua lashing

Time's tongue is long and corrosive
    it has licked rivulets into canyons
        severed the connection between continents
          compelling them to different parts
              of the planet
It has swallowed the ice from polar caps
    only to replace them eons later.

But its effects can be small scale
        can be personal
The glossa action
        removes hair from a man's head
          leaches the colour
            from any that remains

It wearies bones
    sucks the spring from youthful step
        glazes over the ability
            of eyes to see sharply
    damps down the clarity of sound
    as perceived by ageing ears

Even so the heart fights back
    savouring the joy of mere existence
        though eyes have dimmed
        rejoicing more keenly
          the sights of every day

So the age old battle is fought
        by so many
            against time's whiplash instrument
Inevitably it is lost
        but often with grace and dignity

Much as we may wish it
        time's wrackful tongue
            will never disappear
                inside el Supremo's mouth

Prayer of an insomniac

I hate the night
    its cruel claws
Let me flee west
    at the speed of Earth's spin
  stay always
      in late afternoon's wrap
    always ahead
      of night's baleful grasp

Avoid the hours
    of doubt and fear
  avoid the wretched loneliness
      of time in the demi-world
        between wake and sleep
Sidestep being shaken by dreams
      like a rat in the mouth of a terrier
    avoid the dress rehearsals for death

Oh how well I know
      the numbers of the clock face
    know their extended families
      their cruel secrets
    learnt because of the glacial speed
      with which they change places

How I need to avoid
      imprisonment with scores of my uncertainties
        boxed in by overwhelming black cubes of nothingness

Don't let the charm
>	of the first tinge of morning
>		soften my resolve

Let me flee west
>	apace of Earth's spin

Waiting room ritual

The walls of this world of uncertainty
    are slabbed with notices
        soaked in certainty
The perils of whooping cough and diabetes
    sprawl starkly exposed
After the umpteenth reading
    the warnings forfeit
        any literary charm

You sit alone
    wrapped in your inner self

Those about you resemble bees
    lost and directionless
        dozed by fumes
            from apiarist smoker

But it lasts just so long
Infants plunge unconcerned
    into a sea
        of rattling plastic toys

Soon music of different conversations nudges
    above the threshold of awareness
Various melodies
    splash
        against your senses
    now between parent and child
    another across family divides

But again you wait
    along with everyone

Your straw hat sits on your lap
        draws your attention
                to deeply marked lines
            signalling the approach
                of its mortality
        but still with a little time left
                to live out

As waiting continues
        fresh conversations start up
            like grass fires
                spreading across areas
                      previously untouched.

Some are called.

Those waiting proffer a speculative diagnosis
    before the called reach the surgery
        each judgement partnered by a sphere
            of imagined sensations
the rattle of hospital trolleys
a bustle of purposeful white coats
    with shoes clumping
and always
        that particular smell of thoroughness

Such a package
        could await you
    a spin of Fate's old teetotum
                will set the scene
You'll know in time

You check if your phone is turned off

Now the air is filled with different music
Mahler, you guess
       from a PA
    hopefully not his funeral march
The receptionist types furiously
       setting up a counterpoint
            between the rattle of the word processor
                and the sprightly amplified music

Time loses its shape

Any moment
       the slightest event
            a welcome distraction

Tally up those in the queue
       ahead of you
    check your watch
       calculate how late things are running

Move your legs
   so you can stand quickly
      when it's your turn

A bundle of expected questions
       and their answers
           rehearse a woolly path
               through your brain

Something in a far corner
    catches your attention
You almost miss it
   but yes
      now
  it's your turn

       Your name has been called

Messotopia

The beauty of the young
    is more intense as I sense
        the gap between us widening

The tap on the shoulder by some medical necessity
    becomes more frequent

The memory of good times long past
    contorts and shadows

The need to submerge ourself in fine music
    and beautiful writing intensifies

The universal ache for a saner world becomes stronger

The ruling yahoos flaunt their cruel hollowness
        in idiot abandon
The pet food of popular culture mushrooms across our screens
    of varying sizes

Our brains shrink

Our sensitivity fades

So life's chaotic circus trundles along blindly
    on its haphazard way
  the ringmaster having lost control
      or interest
        or both
    disappears from view
the many denizens left to cope
    with whatever acts
  chance
      now left in charge
        calls upon them to perform

Recovering health in a funambulist manner

For me
   here
      for the first time
         high up
   aided by the nearby tent lights
    I look down
       at all the upturned faces

Each step careful
      but confident
      landing precisely where it should
   the rope's gentle sway
      sends a positive chill
         through my bones
Each breath a joy
    each step a satisfaction
   the hazard of a misstep registers
      but precision is now second nature

From what springs
      this unlooked for
         flush of bliss?

Relief in returning from a darker place
    no doubt boosted
      by daily ingestion
    of the regulated number
     of multicoloured pearls
   steeped in magical healing powers.

Meanwhile
    up high
        where I've never been before
            step follows step

Invitingly the rope stretches before me

    Who knows how far

        I cannot see its end

Senior Time

Time to enjoy the taste of food
without feeling the need
    to eat too much.

Time to enjoy the sight of trees
without feeling the need
    to photograph them.

Time to listen to the conversation of birds
without feeling the need
    to record them.

Time to admire the look of a beautiful person
without feeling the need
    to do anything about it.

Time to think wise thoughts
without feeling the need
    to tell anyone.

Time to ponder our own significance
and picture one drop
    of water in a large ocean.

Inarticulatus dotageous

My tongue hunts for words
while my brain sits in a corner
and sulks

Like lively cattle used to freedom
in wide spaces
words give way reluctantly
to being lined up into an orderly
but straggling queue

The long dark passage ahead of them
before seeing light
further inhibits any enthusiasm
for the way forward

Then the words take on
the nature of sheep
leaving a shute
        each leaping
                into
   the air
        alone
                or
with
      another

before settling

    All is over

My shaky communication ended
The bliss of being silent ensues
My brain shuffles out of its chair
and looks around

Song of a retiree

Time's more loosely corseted bosom
    allows us freedom to explore
To us is known the personality
    of every crockery piece we own
The mating call of postman's bike
    has us at mailbox promptly
Letters hardly have time to settle

Almost devoutly our bin is first in place
on collection night
Look no further
for great pools of information are we
News   sport results   seven day weather
we know it all
    ready to pass it to those
who foolishly loiter within range

And so we fuss away our days
and years in detailed guff
until our bodies rebel
calling a halt
to such frenetic vacuity

Then we have to lie or sit
    thinking
Our world opens up new vistas

Countless universes cloud past
the misty cataracts that dim our eyes

Concepts of eons
    infinite in number invade
our faulting brains

Thoughts of people
lives such as ours
 ant-like in numbers and significance
give us pause.

Great pause.

So drawing on wisdom
    flaked together   from all those years
cemented into place by fear
    or by a desperate wish
to be more than a speck in this parade
so gargantuan in size
    we decide,
oh yes
    firmly we do believe
the invention of a God
        seems a pretty good idea.

Saturday morning

Saturday morning
        slides gracefully into place
an oasis from the roughness
        of the rest of the week.

Saturday morning
        thicker newspapers, extra coffee
perhaps a market where you can wander
        seek and gently argue as our forebears
have done for millennia.

Saturday morning
        people walk more slowly
take the time to chat or wave.

Saturday morning
        the sun seems kinder, the breeze more friendly
time not so demanding.

Saturday morning
        if there's an eternity
after we have taken that last high jump
if there's an eternity
        my vote will be for
stretching on for the end of time
        one great big fat never ending

        Saturday morning.

Proposals for the afterlife

I'm going to marry you
    in another life
I missed out this time
    but I'll get you in the next
You know
    somewhere out there
        on one of those countless planets
            in one of those countless universes
    we'll get together
      good and proper
  even if we haven't really met
    this time round
  or we may have known each other for years

No reflection on my arrangement
  this time around
      a most happy entanglement
  but as they nearly said
      Variety is the spice of afterlife

So, in such an afterlife
        we've got to meet up somehow
I picture hoards of dead people somewhere
    trampling this road
        in a purposeless manner
    much like refugees
        streaming out of their bombed home town
But if you're anywhere near me
    I'll spy those legs
        sense that laugh
            feel that lovely enwrapping empathy
In an instant the dust of uncertainty will clear

So dear neighbour
    or long time friend
        or newsreader
    or actress
        or stranger in the train
    or checkout operator
        or any of a host of others
    get ready for it
        as enticing after-lives beckon

www.ingramcontent.com/pod-product-compliance
Lightning Source LLC
Chambersburg PA
CBHW070048120526
44589CB00034B/1599